In the Night Field

In the Night Field

Cameron McGill

Augury Books • Brooklyn, New York

In the Night Field
© 2021 Cameron McGill

ISBN-13: 978-1-936767-65-6

Cover design by Adam Bohannon. Edited by Kate Angus.

Published in the United States of America by:
Augury Books
154 N 9th St #1
Brooklyn, NY 11249
WWW.AUGURYBOOKS.COM
INFO@AUGURYBOOKS.COM

Distributed to the trade by Small Press Distribution / SPD
www.spdbooks.org

Library of Congress Cataloging-in-Publication Data

Names: McGill, Cameron, author.
Title: In the night field / by Cameron McGill.
Description: First edition. | Brooklyn, NY : Augury Books, [2021] |
   Summary: "The debut poetry collection from writer and musician
Cameron McGill"-- Provided by publisher.
Identifiers: LCCN 2020057207 (print) | LCCN 2020057208 (ebook)
   | ISBN 9781936767656 (paperback) | ISBN 9781936767663 (ebook)
Subjects: LCGFT: Poetry.
Classification: LCC PS3613.C4817 I5 2021 (print) | LCC PS3613.
   C4817 (ebook) | DDC 811/.6--dc23
LC record available at https://lccn.loc.gov/2020057207
LC ebook record available at https://lccn.loc.gov/2020057208

FIRST EDITION

for my mother, and for my father

Contents

III.

IV.

V.

The piano stands there in the dark
like a boy with an orchid.

-C.D. Wright

I.

44.6336° N, 86.2345° W

Michigan open your dark umbrella
your benzedrined night sky

Give me the mind slipping from my hands
gravel roads beyond county lines & the rain's understanding
Where I am full as a pupil & miniature
in the moonlight   I have come home

This house in cloudshadow is language
is I empty my pockets & my life
There are twelve rivers inside my body
I drown in eleven of them   One
brings me to you

I keep a small light where the madmen can't
touch it   The dogs can't touch it

The dock's thin arm reaching to the lake drops the moon like a yolk
I let go the dark   that you would come
take me by the hand to a field
I wait now among a stand of pines
so that anywhere I go will be a clearing

40.1164° N, 88.2434° W

I think of youth as one long summer
incorrectly   Mornings the gray of a horse's pink tongue
Farmers calling in the corn from Thomasboro
surrounded by harvests   tall as men gaunting doorways
of train stations   sunburnt & matchless at Logan & Water

I've grown away
slowly like a fingernail   Where is my sister
in her torrential blond   Running skinny in the yard
with the neighbor boy who'd later hang himself

How I didn't try to love him
who torpedoed by sadness & psychiatry chased me home
yelling all his mind at the street
The decrepit limousine our lives had been

Here is a promise the length of my body
that you will take me like a silo   of smoke leaving
the cigarette in my father's hand

The dreams I had forgive me
When spring's tornadoes came we raced
with paper to the basement
& drew them

MOONFLOWER

I think of you where the forest swallows light,
where crosses on the highway are religion's limits.
The deer carcass calls to the crows.
Tires on wet pavement scatter them
to what lent-purple light is left in the west.
They settle in eaves like vowels from the dead.
This awful forest, home to dark engines—
to those who speak in hoarded consonants,
to *Spring*, which isn't Latin for *things un-die*.
What are you growing in me, God,
where your green apron darkens?
Did I always close to the sun
before there even was one?

44.6336° N, 86.2345° W

This is not a nightmare this is how the world looks
in a forest at night   phantasmagoric
in the canopy   The sound of sleet ticking
on bark that quakes like tuning forks
in the crowns of pine   Crowns like the heads of waves
seen by no one

but my father & me
In the four o'clock dark   a fluency of branches
swimming at the window means I wake in blue
The room a vanity with rain on it

Downstairs he rises with his cough
His small lamp hung in the dark   Who smokes must be
talking to himself   There is a freighter skulking full of ore
pounding sleepknots to Charlevoix

This distant country called me home
Why have I only brought it adjectives

I try to sleep
She is not next to me I cannot   put my hand on her back
I have only a stormful   of trees in the dark

AFTER WORK

My father split his attention
with an icepick. Crushed four fingers
of a tumbler, lit ten cigarettes
like birthday candles, blew them out.

He offered me the olives—each round
bitter, salt and ethyl on my tongue—a truce
without words. I understood

what was agreed upon
those nights when two
unlikely things were forced together—
I slipped the slick red hearts from their cavities.
I was a kid; I was helping.

44.6336° N, 86.2345° W

Morning expands one rib at a time
speaks through the pinktops of pines   On the porch
I write to a friend whose mother has passed
Blue fog is a doe that startles
at my cough   I drink black water from its eye

This isn't about halfdreamt things
The veil over the lake about to boil a man
It's too quiet to answer anything but the tonguecolors
of the east   fernlight slices from a mandoline

My words are bad acreage
I think of taking my friend's grief   holding it
above my head & wading out   It is clear I can see the sand
I tell myself this is helping   this is what the heart looks like working

Each step   the outbreath
There is a boat & a man moving his line
To the still dark he's throwing   longer & longer threads

40.1164° N, 88.2434° W

I don't care what you say the moon
was a fishhook catching the lip   of an orange slice
I wore over my teeth   The stars
porchlights on strange & unnamed mountains
pulled at the stitching of dogwoods   or my mouth

which spelled the corduroy of peeling paint
on a First Street balcony   I dreamt
large wrecks rising slowly from the Great Lakes
satellites hot & sinking
in the grand marble halls of train stations

I used to think street names took you there—
Colorado Paris Ashley   I believed this
as hot air balloons lifted over Champaign   as I watched
for the pulling of the chaindownfire & the rise
of lanterns in the dark to Europe
Thomasboro Rantoul   Everywhere

a green ocean of backyard   My mind
like the spine of a splayed book   I was young
the way a glass of water bends a spoon
The way aphids in moonlight are more blue
Any way

COUNTING DOWN THE ERA

The Space Race reached my body
in the *Challenger*. A classroom in Champaign.
America in the sun and ten times headed for the moon
from the Cape. That birthday candle thrusting in blue cake,
pushing earth away for seventy-three seconds.
We had just counted down. We had all counted down.

How it fireworked wrong and came apart like sun-
light daggered through the trees and windows of a house
where months before at our kitchen table
my mother on the phone using a strange voice, and me hearing
only her questions, the answers changing her face,
hung up and said her father had died.

I watched for correction—
my sister running in the yard,
clouds like chandeliers through the trees.
She existed in the garden, in dogwoods, through the sprinkler,
and in sundown on poplars at the incline of the road.
Her hair like house lights coming on over the fence.

My mother and I existed, and the fly on the table
existed in a darkness that cracked and splashed
its wet-blue-life, speckled pink like robins' eggs
dropping from the pines.

The footage of her face kept happening—

surrendering to her sadness made it mine.
Then nothing, except my sister

walking to the house not knowing anything
about dying, and my fear in beginning to understand it,
so that I knew it later in that classroom
when there was nothing again. And nothing fell.

Surely no one had survived but us.
There was a teacher on the mission, they said.
She would have been the first. A long silence—
till mine, with hair on fire and a voice swallowing
all of the Atlantic, told me to turn it off.

41.9740° N, 87.6782° W

I'm less the buildings I used to live in
& more the strangers passing in their windows—
the woman dancing with her baby   holding him high
a man carrying laundry to the bedroom with a beer

I return your shadow
to where I found it in me   beside chimneys
on Damen Avenue   in an alley piling breath into January

I live in too much silence—
there needs to be someone in the car the room the bed   The world
in its heartbreak of mastery wants me undone

To come here knowing nothing
should want to speak   except the wind & frost on the grass
in shadows of trees on Winnemac   This all starts to sound the same—
the city the block
my assurances   The deficits they make of memory

Yesterday I met the woman I'd lived with for years
My remembering a bath
her knees islands in the cooling water   I'm afraid
describing things ruins them   That's not true It was me
who asked what the body wanted & didn't
listen for the answer

DRUNK WITH ZODIAC

for Cyd

Taurus charges in the dark like Oregon,
horns the width of this beer with a moon.

I forget where I live, keep repeating your name.
Its gray dissolve in rain at night is fair.

Paradise Ridge fogged in breath, my bad health
and the pines' ice-lungs. Orion is a butterfly

turned on its wing, pinned against boredom
and black paper. Our bodies cut askew,

shiver up and to the west, ricocheted
and charcoal-burnt as maps. The myth

of beasts unseen, animations on the night:

> Fronds of bracken hung like hair
> of the subway cellist, legs spread and hugging;

> the boxer's head thrown back,
> nose bloody gushing stars; the young

> woman breastfeeding who's fallen asleep;
> gaunt man seated, finger raised, recalls

> certain beauty of youth; your birthmark
> like a thin fox torn across the sky.

> And what of that shooting one—my twin
> whose streak shirks blur—the runner

> giving chase, whose feet cannot be seen.

It's no use trying not to die in this dream
Streetlights the gold chargers
on my kitchen table   My family surrounds me like statues
in East City Park Their eyes   pockmarks on the sidewalk
filled with rainlight & the sleepcrawl of branches

A man smokes in his doorway downwind
on Blaine   arm swinging like a singlechain thurible
Everything the size of a cathedral   His eyes
bedsprings lonely bodies fall onto in dark basements
Face translucent raw as newborn rabbits

I know myself by the things that scare me
Veins humming in my hands are raised
dark roads   I have been holding
tight onto everything

The night is numbered
in a forest of sharps & flats
in a register climbing wet mirrors   Inside me
a silo fills with rain
I sing into it

FOREST EXERCISES

I am the son of the bird fire that has no eyes but sings to itself after
waiting alone and silent in the alien wood.
-W.S. Merwin

I. MY WILD FAMILY

Come down when you hear the chainsaw,
he says as I leave the house.
Our time together, best with work.
Morning through the slatted boards, cuticles of light.
I remember him before anger sharpened
as teeth from patterns of wear. His blood's rough edges
run in my wrists. Mice gnawing kindling in the shed—
their god, a hole in the wall to Michigan.

I leave a stream of wet sunlight on the ferns and my stare in the woods.
Music through the walls, classical and muddled.
A doe ten feet away looks up, chews. Doesn't move.
Her eyes shine green as a level's liquid.
A fawn uneven on the path.

His machine grabs in the distance, and my wild family scares.
Father, we bite at trunks and our tongues.
We are slow as trees to forgive.
I am your prince of silence
walking toward the noise in your hands.

II. MY LEAVING AND HIS

I've learned to listen
for the door slam, the engine's turn.
In the woods, leaves are still
and thin green faces.
I lean at the jamb of the shed,
my body ages uncontrollably.
Early June, dawn and the sounds begin. The world
unfolding its map-tight sleep.
The compass points inward
to the knives of stars, to cardinals of forgetting.
Say, *A son's no thing but a map to likeness.* Or don't.
Have I become the way you look to me?
A bird calling to another of its kind—
the answer begins to rain.
It is raining in the darker parts of my body.

III. DARK CARGO

This is the one where I disappear
into syllables of my name, curse handfuls of sparrows
in the poplar, make my body the long thin tongue
of a fly-line licking Michigan dust from leaves.
         I listen to your body speak—

1,000 coughs of convalescents
pushing out a death-air. The black of wet trunks
like men in long coats, their hands leathered in the rain and quick.
I am going somewhere three sentences from safety.
         Who will carry me back?

Rain from April's dark strata
shivers on the leaves as we walk the gravel drive.
There is no dream between us, only my eyes,
two wetted envelopes battening the dusk.
         The license your silence gives me to love you.

My arms, the handles of a wheelbarrow you fill
with hard earth. How we move ourselves,
how we clear the beach, pulling everything green.
Take my hands that you might understand me.
         That I might open to darkness.

46.7324° N, 117.0002° W

I've become an issue of tense
I am   we were   you are
the missing part the missed the two
extra buttons sewn inside my shirt   I press them
now between my ribs

& snow falls on lights of the silos
lengthens wintergrass in my hair
My breath leaves like trainsmoke   dissipates
as lights come on in high windows of the jail

I say *happiness* out loud   that it would be enough
of a prescription   Branches & fire escapes darken
Night slides down the throat of a steeple
I've lost the center   There is no center
Only administrations of houselights & a qualification of bells

Nothing rhymes with *orange* in English except a memory—
a woman with cat eyes buried in moonlight
on a rooftop in Manhattan when she reached   for my hand

Carry me to that woman's ear   to the dimple
of her lower back   that smelled of lilacs & Maldon salt
For now I call November to the sky   all its constellations—
those just being born those just now dying

MYTHOS

'I have a bird in my head,' he says. 'I can't get it out.'

-Yannis Ritsos

Mother, I am wrong—
we are not from stone, but my memories
make hard things of beauty.
     There is a small bird that lives inside me
telling everything backwards to my birth.
There, there, he says and scares
from a wooden table where a chair's been pushed away.
He moves between my ribs, holds them like branches
with a voice that calms horses, like the dark boards of dreams.
In a field outside the town of my youth, he waits
like a young widow for sleep.
     The name he calls my blood is yours.
He leaves his work in the corners of my eyes,
in drawings on the walls of my mouth
where a man stands in a field, an ornament to moonlight.
Sometimes he lies down, others
he takes a knee, a bath, a life.

II.

WILLIAM BLAKE & THE ETERNALS

after Van

I was a late arrival here.
Years spent pulling my voice apart
like a wishbone for song. I started a band
to meet girls and metaphysicians.
We called ourselves William Blake & The Eternals.
Something was missing.
I sang, *gulls*, it sounded like *girls* in an English accent.
I sang, *What is emptiness to what is no longer empty?*
We had no hits, obviously.
They dropped us in late spring
with the noise of a Coffee Mate clicking.
They'd *done the numbers,* and *No.*
It took a sleepless year in a stranger's basement
on Monticello not to kill myself.
I sang, *I've done the numbers, and no.*
Our only song had been a poem about a man
holding a lantern at the end of a long hallway
lined with books and firewood.
He haunted me, as did his horse,
which all night would shift its legs,
stamping gently the floorboards.
The song was called "Farriers." I sang it
only once in Montana, in late-August '89,
as my father and I stood in a field
at dusk, and with the fog holding everything,
a yoke of starlight lifted from him,
weightless and lifetimes ago.

AN AGREEMENT

From a loose nail in the wall
I hang a picture of two silos filled with moonlight.
I imagine rain through the streetlights behind them.

Their inner reaches stretch before my birth. A blur
at the edge walking out of frame
says, *Filled with joy is a possibility, wife is a question.*

I stand in the room like a man balancing
in the back of a box-truck his life.
I run my fingers along the inside of September,
remove strings from the piano, silver hairs from my temple.

In the silos' shadow, I want understanding
and the empire of memory
separate. Staggering, their output of echoes.

I can't help it, I ask them, *Why?*
My tall silences. They say everything
being here. By not answering.

41.9740° N, 87.6782° W

When I wake your voice   falls through me
Years I drew from it on Ravenswood
on Winchester   Your breath no longer written on my chest
I get closer to the earth on my knees to hear

Tap the window for the sound my body makes
on its reflection   The sky is forced to listen
I walk further each day toward the strange
austerity my heart makes of reason

You are a light I keep pressed against me The notes
of dead keys abandoned in my body

I take the walls apart a brick at a time
Stack sections of sky behind my eyes
When I close them your language   is a trespassing

That day we took a boat down the river   Did it empty
into the lake Did the Manitous lay before us
like tired cubs in the sun Did we stay through the small hours

My memories have found ways to travel
in darkness I can hear them now   I move between rooms
called forgetting my dreams

I don't know where the day ends
but that it does when I try   to sleep When I imagine you are
& so pretend   to feel close

DINNER WITH ZODIAC

It must be the work of early-career astronomers
to catalog Neruda's night sky full of roses.
I sway in the street when looking at the moon-tops of pines.
I am an ox pissing against flowers in a park, and quiet
is light years arriving on a wet wink of leaves.
Rhododendrons, their purpled eyes searching my face.

It is June; I am a dragon
in a twelve-year cycle. According to the placemat in my pocket,
You are eccentric and your life complex. Really,
I am selfish like the rooster, candid like tigers.
I need to avoid the dog.

On nights when the moon fills its ballrooms,
it startles streetlights in the folds of women's dresses.
Memory won't stop happening to me.
I stand at the sink and cry spent horses.
I have held hands in the dark with a rabbit.
Tell me what to do—*Marry a rat late in life.*
There is no animal for the year we meet.

CRUELTY WOULD POSSESS ME

if I didn't find everything beautiful.
A man calls repeatedly from the tree line for *Leo*.
The sky, a ladder from the pines. Dusk climbs
methodic down the ribbon of a dog's throat.
The up-pitched call nailed to the walls of May.
My sign named in the evening. A *Leo*
gone missing, and the man's voice
more annoyance than worry. I am
the only *Leo* it reaches, leaning in this shed.
Tornado-light in the maples. *Leo*, the word
bayoneting the blue. *Leo*, the sky
your night-sugared handful. *Leo*, shake out
your gone-silent chambers. This human,
calling and calling *Leo* to the painted rain.
Leo, these shadow-stained wings on the road.
Leo, what bruises we are on the world. Alone,
I listen to a dog called home and want to obey.
Leo, my father's voice like looking at a light
whose shape remains after I close my eyes.

FOREST EXERCISES

IV. LEVELING

August. Frankfort. Leveling the birches.
Ribbons on trunks marked for cutting.
You aren't worried about their chances.
High up, thin trees struggle for light—
They've grown toward stronger ones.
I convince you to save a paper birch
I'd climbed as a child.
                              What things!
This forest is not our way to talking.
Above the road you kneel, shout my help for tools
and the wheelbarrow, which I empty at your knees.
You work in the noises at dusk like a factory
shutting down, one light at a time.
                              Father,
I've grown toward you and away from myself.
My shoes fill with sky.
I will not make a lifetime of decisions easy on you,
though I'd take your hand on my back for words.

All your wagering me in the world
has only hurt the world. I love
          differently now—
the names I call myself when you no longer care
to be the one I answer to.

V. LIKENESS

Talking feels canceled when I stand alone
in the forest. Mother, your thinness is a letter
to my worry. I watch you work in the garden.
I confuse solitude with loneliness.
My hair is also gray kisses at sundown.
A doe strafes the ridgeline until lost
in the thicket, only snapping brush.

God undressed in an arbor of madness;
I am his mannequin's shadow.
My eyes empty the last clip of daylight
into the forest, and quietly
the rain on leaves leaves leaves clean.

You have tried to make me yours;
I think of the bones you broke to bring me here.
I promise, I am trying to love the world.
It is not impossible. Here,
place your flowers on the sill inside me.

VI. RETURNING HOME, I BEGIN

Seasons are born wet too, and night
facedown on the lawn like young drunks.
I hear high school boys wolving
the woods, blissful in their immutable odd power.
They hunt the night, cocky and occluded.
I lie on the ground under heat lightning.
Girls scream; it rains into me.

I'm standing in a sunken room
with a purple cup, following the purr
of my young mother's voice.
            Everything's capitalized:
God, my Grapejuice-Tongue,
Firelight Shadows like Cubist Birds,
my Voice thrown like Confetti
to your Hands reaching to brush the Hair
from my Forehead. Mother, Everyone
keeps sinking. My arrangement of
language is false.
            Darkness
is like sleeping when you can't. I can't.
I was born. You taught me
kindness; it is not the easy way.
Father cut the cord, he told me. I bled.
He wishes he'd left more. Youth,
your wet mirror blurs with my hand.
My age is a hand; I have forty hands.

All myth begins with the possessive.
I'm under the maples now, Mama,
follow my voice—
Sorry is the present tense of I *can't help it*,
the past tense of *Why?*
If you say I'm like father, I am.
If you say I'm your child, or nothing.
Can I still come home to be it?

44.6336° N, 86.2345° W

Here I am being something better than rain
Sitting with a cigarette at the back of everything   Apparitioned
clouds stain my teeth   Gray a vulture coming for me
Mama I've shown it too much
Headlights blur the shine of does' eyes
their shadows cancel branches

There my voice brings nothing back
from Beulah   but the purples of January
I am sick of nature   human or otherwise
Where is a kindness I can mimic

Take my memory scraped raw by lake rock
& latitude Take my nerves   knife gouges in the linoleum

When I sat on the dock this morning asking
for compassion I pretended   the waves were breaths
repeating *Yes*   I saw the heart for what it is
a noisemaker

Of all the things I'm not   I am certain
of meridians reaching from forgiveness & love
That somewhere in the distance they meet

I DIDN'T DISAPPEAR

There is a god of small thunder
in my chest, serving commandments:
whiskey, birds, women, feed the strays.
His appetite grows as I watch Manitou twins
or breakers in Grand Traverse. He reminds me
blood is still red without air, and Escanaba
is a decent drive if you've been drinking.
I listen to him hungry mornings, walking
Michigan dawns, sleeves of ash
tipping the arm of my cigarette. The dog
bark of newspaper hits my screen door
like a bad decade. When I was younger,
the winds of Montana, the winds
of Grayling, tore pages from my hair.
One hundred miles into the future I still die
in a field of baled hay, longing to have seen
Livingston one last time.
                              Take me back:
Leelanau, west arm of northern Bay,
Big Sky where graves are horses
with no tack on a farm by a windmill that slows
to the good eye. I didn't disappear.
My body became a flower
in the fist of a thick book. Find me
the mouth of a river. I am loose gravel,
a road tracing a mountain onto night.
The afterlife, two currents against each other.
The god has stopped. I am still
a climber of fences, a traveler
stepping forward, a salmon
killing itself to get back.

COMPENDIUM FOR KEEPING IT TOGETHER

In the shed full of bloodroot seed:
ball-peen hammers, sawhorses, brooms.
I tack my list *No Rules* to the wall.
A single bulb scatters mice to *Make strange*
bags of kindling. *Be reckless* My youth,
memories cleft between the mind and desk.
I tremble papers and *Lose reason*
carve initials into slatted boards.
Outside, fat crows in gravel
brutalize the morning. *Leave gaps*
          No booze for two weeks,
and I wonder about the Olympic deck cleaner
high up on the shelf, *Take risks* the pain
of peanut butter jars filled with nails,
Chop beginnings sixteen saws
and the damage I could do
to this wooden shed. *It is not your right*
to feel powerless Sunlight's a puncture wound
inside me that tries to spread.
As if they see me in here,
I wave to no one.
What things are not Give me those
happy wounds, you slouch of a sun.

I TAKE

the Lord's name into them, my hands—
where it is dark and my grandmother cannot hear
the curse I learned from my uncle
who lives in her basement of rotted apples.

I take the mourning doves in their right mind
on New Street where they print low aches in my ears.
Wearing my grandfather's ruck, unused since the war,

I take her arm through the raspberry rows
with a wooden bowl on my head.
Her handkerchief, my red pilot in summer.

The dry socket of August.

She takes the fruit, makes it bleed
on her teeth. Takes the outwash of seeds
staining everything. Takes my hands,
their slight quick vote for happiness.

WHEN THE HORSEMAN CAME FOR
MY GRANDMOTHER'S MIND

I.
Her hair was a gathering of skeleton keys
hanging on a workbench in the basement of a house
in Glen Ellyn in the dark. She was stuffing twenty-dollar bills
into light fixtures and coffee cans.

II.
In Missoula, you think we're in Pearl Harbor,
that I am my sister. You ask for Gershwin—
Cam used to play the piano before he went to Vietnam.

You might have waged the winter
as that single tree in the parking lot—
I thought for sure the dark red blooms
were gloves against the snow and horse.

The rider in black, sun-snuffed and skim-milk eyes.
Fingers chewed to burnt matchsticks.
You tell him, *No,* you are not ready.
The mask he wears, wet.

The human heart is battery of the mind.
I give my hands to the muzzle.
My baby picture bedside, a shirt that said *Kid.*
With your love, you'd name me later.

You said I was yours. *Take him,
the boy. He knows what to do.*
I did not know.
I stood in the breath of the mare.

III.
I used to dance the big bands.
The dresses were long.
Russell?
Did you see him?
I don't remember my name.
I recognize you.
I grew up on a farm.
When father died it smelled like this.
Brooms. Wet dog.
Is that you, father? Cobweb?
That field outside looks cold is anyone else?

ACKNOWLEDGMENT

The spinet in its dust.
Picture frames leave their shapes as he lifts them,
visible between piles of lyrics.
Inside the bench—horn charts,
news clippings, an ocean stone.
Curtains in the next room like centuries.
Sunlight shows the keys he played last—
dead ones, their shoulders slumped.
Watch as he sits, adjusts a picture of his family.
He's running a finger across their faces,
wiping it on his jeans.

PHARAOH

You are asleep,
arms crossed upon your chest.
I whisper to you
blue in TV-light,

collect your breath
in jars, shelve them
inside me.

Nothing waits
except the filth under your nails.

Tomorrow, a doctor
will search your body
for wrong languages dying
to preserve themselves
like kings.

44.6336° N, 86.2345° W

Spirits passing through hair & the linen
shirts of young men smoking in the park
They dream the undergarments   of crabgrass & the despair of leaves
Dewclaws & the milked undersides of cottonwoods
are also dreamt   They sweep

cobwebs hanging in pint glasses
speak for pollen & the dead   At Point Betsie
decommissioned moonlight in the Fresnel lens
says the heart when the mouth is cold

I listen by watching   the breakwater's chains
lakers laden with ore   the raspberry's wet curfew
against the calamine of a stripped birch
Behind everything waves   concrete gray & unplaced on faces

I know you're there
Say my life is still   here & reckless
I'll open the canned moonrise with my teeth

INVENTIONS TOWARD PLEASURE

Cardinal points drum down slaked
waves to crumble at my feet. The soul is
when the body's inside looks the same
as out, only behind glass. My feet
underwater, mirror clear. I read once
when humans die off, so too will
sadness—our second invention toward
pleasure. Some things insist more than
we do—clutches of birds V-ing in a
southern panic, last-light tearing like
lions of color at the trees from dunes to
pier. Beauty, our first—wild word in
summer, dangerous perennial. Our
bodies made both—helpless pilots
amongst a shake of pine, tiers upon tiers
of career-ending violets.

BECAUSE I DID NOT DIE

I was born in the whisper of a coccyx bone.
Smelled of pennies at 8:12 AM on a Tuesday
in August, wrapped in a blanket of apples
and a boy-blue hat. Flowers filled vases in the room.
My father thought of the force it took to cut the cord,
wondered what they did with its dried fruit.

My body, a window so clean a bird flew into it.
In Urbana and silence, I was held into the world—
first tick on the wall of original joy
is coming from nothing into all this.
What our bodies make of need, they tell you later.
How I started taking right away.
Grandma saying, *All men come from the same place,*
some it softens on the way out.

FOLLOWING INSTRUCTIONS

What part of her body was under my fingernails
as I sifted handfuls over the flowerbed?
My shoes passing shivers to blades of grass
that kept her ash on their tongues
like shadows sunlight couldn't shake.
Her body, a coarseness; I considered a spoonful.
Said *flower* over and over, meaning *her name*
until something bloomed.

I left her by the black rock beneath the blue spruce,
inside the unlit pagoda lantern rusting by the wooden shed,
and on roses, their petals in gray motes.
I carried syllables of her body like a coffee can of coins.

Giving her back to the flowers—
saying *delphinium* assured the future, where hands
are more than sieves raining seeds to a field.
And standing, I watched them sink.
Her hair in my nails; nose in my eyes;
four chambers of the heart, my mouth.
I left some in the bird feeder,
gave her to the skyway like string in a beak.

Closing down the house,
I left fingerprints on the sink,
on the wall as I switched off her kitchen light,
the door handle I turned to leave.
My own face. Dorothy,
I followed the instructions.
I wanted to touch everything once.

III.

TO BONEYARD CREEK

A sky blue as corpses follows you—
thin ribbon of rock and shoe, beer can and needle.
In Urbana, you're no more than a tangled skein
at Goodwin and Green. A wet dark belt
threading the waist of my town. Crossing Third
at Healey, limping toward my old high school.
You were always something decrepit in me.
On smokers' hill, breath spirits ivy through the chain-link fence,
crows in the oak like cold Mission figs,
limbs bending over Lynn, outstretching fingertips.
I keep you around my chest, close to the darkest blood.
I want to say enough. Memory, enough.

Would you raise me like fat balloons in summer—
hot air over Hessel in the eye of a cloud shouting *fire*?
That seventh birthday, the unfilled piñata.
My friends, their thin bodies
swinging at the gangly dusk. Blindfolded
blank faces, anonymous reservoirs.
Several are dead. Their bodies,
willows. Their names,
petrichor. Their eyes,
your water in stages of thaw. I forget
what I meant to say for the ends of their lives.

At school, I could only joke
at the terrible way priests sang in monotone,
remembering every fit held in—my fourth-grade friend

St. Mark, turning red as he laughed silently,
tears streaming his face, upturned to the clean
light of the stained glass. The Stations.
No small divinities, the past.
The bulk of our coverage fell away.

I want everything that has already
gone to return to me,
so I can tell what it meant.
I might be wrong.

Let me remember my address, my landline,
the names of my friends' dead mothers.
My uncles staggering the Boneyard
as scarecrow-clothed wretches.
My mother, sister, and I in the car,
father skulking the miles home on foot after Christmas.
His nights long as drags from discontinued brands.
He moves in the sheet cake silence,
teeters in snow on the edge of no greatness.

Let me remember subtraction—
the qualities I strike from what is not man in me.
The heart forever saying yes,
floods and moves on.
Floods and moves on. Against the world
I hold a light. We are thin together.
Sit still, it says. *Wait,* it means.
There is sun on your face;
you haven't done so wrong.

Stucco-white in ecru open fields,
west Champaign, your long-wide breaths of avenue.
My room at the south corner of the house,
small wooden desk with drawers
where I kept my moon-foolish notes.
In the yard, spine-straight cypresses
fixed their green hair for school.
My mother on the phone in the kitchen,
her banquets of laughter I ate on the stairs.

There was a fire when I was young,
started by painters in the attic above my room.
We stood on the lawn long-faced,
Ralph Stanley's twang through the crumbs of AM.
At the intersection of two dead presidents,
tires whispering onto wet brick. The air
a black-licorice tang of fennel on my tongue.
Dogwoods cotton-white and pink shot hot.
The house looking east from McKinley in the rain,
a blur of streetlamps in place of my birth.

Nothing's good enough.
I return my body to the Boneyard:
past the drunk's house, where a French horn struggles
with a waltz. The man trying to dissolve
into the old parts of his skill, playing what his ear remembers
the wind makes beautiful again.
Past dogs biting at bees in a construction site
where Burnham Hospital used to stand.
My grandfather died there shortly after I was born,
and we floated miles together along the creek,
spirits sluiced blue to the sky's wet culverts.

Past the wing-flutter of someone shaking
out a rug against a wrought iron railing
on the porch of a clapboard house on Green.
That apartment on First Street
where I'd held you from behind in a small room
white with morning sun, and the whole of Illinois
floated like a moth in the light
as you asked me to fill you up, and I wanted to
with everything.

Past men with laudanum tongues
pressed to the wind's mouth,
confessing the necessity of flasks.
Shoulders shrug the runoff from reservoirs.
Pinch of happiness I send to the world,
hoping it returns hungry. I still run
against the question mark of your body.
Whatever prescience comes, I say *Okay*,
and trace my fingers along its stone.
My slumped Leviathan,
this is where I mistake the cruise ship for the tub.
I spit in the sinew of the city,
drink beer from a paper bag,
piss on the trunk of the tree I felled
whose ribs are stacked against the night.
Whose magnets of green fire charge the grass.
The slingshot moon. My own voice—
a red twist in the wind,
a thread pulled through sparrow-air.
I name it after myself: Cameron Read, Dreamless,
Church Street, Midnight West Side Park.
I might be wrong.

If *domum* is Latin for *home*, Champaign is *domum*
for *nothing waits for me.* You are ten dreams away.
My only argument, beauty...
and the self... and the father... and the pilot light.
I am the son calving. No matter.

~ᴑ

Don't you know memory is the mansion—
I stand alone in its ballroom,
darkness twirls. On the wall, a painting of a field,
and in the field, a woman gathering her dress
by a well. Stones tower into ground.
A basket of wash at her feet.
She is looking toward a river.

~ᴑ

Where are you, my little light?
On the ripple, on the bridge,
in the vanity of that corner room?
Boneyard, I've become the shadow
of all the colors inside you.
On the days I tremble your name behind me,
tucked in the folds of my shirt, beneath the linings of my shoes—
I place you between myself and the world. I am learning
I cannot paint sadness on everything.
It is simply not the truth.

I count the days I've been alive—
the days I followed you back home
until you ended, and the days you lit my leaving.
I am from whatever you are.
Dare I say you were enough.

IV.

THIS DREAM

Nothing scares me anymore
except the past tense—
how you walked through my sleep
     like the streets we'd lived on.

     I was with you again—
fingers of light through the curtains in Maam. Little joy.
Cold washrags on a line at dawn, my eyes
bloodshot-blue, still as a frozen swing.
     Our map a graded paper on the bedside table.

     Campbell's at Croagh Patrick in Murrisk, and Clare
Island curled like a sleeping child. You'd never turn me away.
The ruins in Antrim, that look on your face
     when you said, *There is no tower.*

     Memory's a long rope I pull through myself.
A cracked door, its wild slit of light. And shadow
under eyes like currants in a paper bag.
My forefinger and thumb to sockets, and silent
     I dress. At the kitchen sink,

     I hear my name—
your tenor from the empty living room.
Sadness rings inside me like a pretty bell. Every morning
you subtract yourself from the dark. And the world
     opens like your arms, gets it wrong.

THE ORPHAN TALKING TO HIMSELF
IN THE DARK

I cannot be trusted
to do the dishes on a regular basis or change
burnt-out lightbulbs in the bathroom.

I kill hobo spiders in the tub,
let shower steam lift from my body the spirit—
its molt slipping through the cracked window.

Linoleum sweats under my toes; I want to lie down.
The Midwest begins its gray sentence, and the mirror
surreals my face when I paint it with my palm—

I'm a blurred canyon of pink and hair.
My ribs stick out like bent pencils
tucked longways under the skin.

I am divers hovering black lakes.
I am what drags the Doo Lough.
The way people go mad.
The burnt cities' coercions—
Stay in bed. Write Jonas in Paris.
Go to Ireland with Cydney,
lean in a doorway.

I am the thin match
you scratch against the world.

THE ORPHAN

I call you Orphan, orphan. You are ill.
　　　　-Sylvia Plath

I. STANDING WITH A HORSE ON INISHMORE, THE ENDING STARTS

Aran Islands, County Galway

The soft anvil of its head gave
to your hands through the fence.
Bad weather's maturation in the West—
we stand from the road on a farm in thin rain.
Your secret alphabet with that machine of animals—
eyes, black stones from the North Sound,
voicing your hand along its meadowed nose.
The Orphan wanting to leave you, and I
don't know what makes a thing fair
any more than rain cares about animals.
You spoke in a voice used with children.
My eyes made ships of clouds and sailed them
to a woman in the distant field.
You offered your palm to the jowls,
cupped the chew of its mouth,
scaled the mountain of its head—
a burren between eyes. I wore wool and wine
and watched the grass bend. A noise
startled in the field.

Remain for me at that fence,
arm extended on Aran.
Seabirds shadowing the field. How many
names I've given my remembering—
Junebug, tourist, Cydney at a wall
in Ireland. Your face, when it turned
to me, had the look of a new mother—
relief, though mostly awe
at what was yours and couldn't say its love.

II. ALONE, MORNING IN MURRISK, YOU CLIMB CROAGH PATRICK

Murrisk, County Mayo

Silence was the language of the clear blue.
Our separate sleep in the rented room.
You rose early for the mountain,
The Orphan held his apology, turned like a breath to the wall.
My tongue struck flint on the dawn,
and there was no dream.

꩜

You stand at the summit in a frame for saints.
Clare Island's a slumped drunk,
and that white chapel atop the mountain waits
in a tongue of sunlight that drives all the snakes wild.
You keep your pact with Patrick.
You'd passed the strictest believers
climbing shoeless on their hands and knees.

꩜

Say something down the mountain for me.
I'm waiting for you at Campbell's with a beer.
Across the street, Behan's famine memorial—
a coffin ship twisting hunger in the park.
Orphan in the corner cleaning his nails with a nail.
School children crossing the road to play
in the grass are tiny brightened ghosts
warming everything. Their laughter
fine as decaying violets.
They give the sculpture no thought
until starting a game of tag
where hunger becomes *home*. Somebody yells
safe. Everyone agrees.

III. ON ACHILL, WHERE JIM RYAN TOLD US TO GO, THE ORPHAN DOESN'T PROPOSE

Achill Island, County Mayo

Away from the cliff, below the road,
a cairn marking the death of someone young,
a traveler. *She loved this island.* The language
of sunken drumlins in Clew Bay—
bloodbaths of blue sky and the shipwrecked
galleons of green. We were terns on the edge.
This is where The Orphan should have asked you.
This is where I should have asked you.
Our coveting the woman back home instead.
Our haunted restless jamped enamora. Love,
my division of labor, and I your sick twin
squinting in the sun. Your smile in our picture
for Jim, to prove we'd taken his advice.
Why couldn't he have told me to be good?

IV. AT KILMAINHAM GAOL, THE ORPHAN TRIES ON
A CELL FOR YOU

Dublin, County Dublin

My only revolution was selfishness.
We queued an hour to be led inside
the jail in early daylight. The Orphan lagging
behind the tour, taking photographs,
ducking into cells. The youngest inmate ever held
was five years old, arrested for stealing
a length of chain. He didn't have
a cell of his own. In a fist that held
sunlight, we stood in the courtyard,
long-shadowed where Connolly was shot,
gangrenous and bound to a chair.
(He couldn't stand.) There was no mercy
in mid-May. The guide spoke of the Easter Rising.
I found a Joseph with my last name
in a glass case, The Orphan's greasy fingerprints.
I'd left him at the window
to find you, alone with no blindfold,
still standing in the courtyard's bright sun.
You made all the deaths worthwhile.
Can that be?

V. FROM HORN HEAD, WE TAKE A FINAL PHOTOGRAPH

Dunfanaghy, County Donegal

The Orphan holds his spirit like a thrush
until it's gifted to the wind
outside Patsy Dan's. The bay sucks its teeth
in low tide. Sheephaven recedes to Tory Sound.
A dog pulls at a fish carcass.
We walk the stout-like muck,
waylaid weeds in an acreage of seabed and bone.
The Orphan mad with brevity, and the world
beyond my reach—the other woman
and the green-fire hills. Sun crowning Horn Head.
And farther out, The Orphan slips as surf
to somewhere colder, more unknown.
We sit in the high grass watching the gears
of ocean turn toward Ireland's edge.
Only you are looking at the camera.
The North Atlantic. Everything ends here—
in my small notebook too, it ends.
Right at this page.
Right here.

Before you move away, our friends throw you a party.
They ask I send pictures; I include this one.
Send the early joys and the late.
Ireland is four dreams away, a country that forgets me.
But *you* are larger than that—
the bells in all my towers, still.

V.

MY TOWN

I made a little town
the last time I saw you
standing in the window
of our apartment.
No one else lives there.
There are houses
made of hungry rivers,
churches of mercury
working your face down
to me in the courtyard.
And my little town burns.
First, at the outskirts,
then cemeteries,
squares, and streets.
The guitars and beds.
There is a man
at his kitchen table
finishing a letter.
Smoke billows
from his window.
He stands,
moves toward the door.
Does he sit back down?

43.6790° N, 114.3741° W

That cloud   a ghosthorse in the larch
the halfsword of its neck lowering under the Pioneers
I watch the barren side of Baldy
fog lifting from Wood River on the first day of snow
as workers race to finish a house

Across Buss Elle a woman sweeps her stoop
Her face a screen of moths
teeth glistening like new decks of cards
Her broom without the straw is just a stick

at dusk   Breath leaves my body & becomes
the ether of streetlamps   hoarfrost on a clockface
I won't call anything the moonlight
or anything that moves in it   a shadow

I'm surrounded
by telephone poles & the wires of branches
by the mountain & the calling fork
& silently   the ruined horse slips the night field

Hundreds of nails driven through a plywood roof
point the rustway of stars
A sparrow took apart its nest in the eaves
I did not drink today

DISTANT COUNTRY

Memory's as fair as it has to be.
You are the handle of a door opening
to a ballroom lit with fireflies. I live in there
like moths caught in a stack of glasses,
a dream slipped into the West. In the dark
I say *No* to whatever love
                      I've promised strangers.

I meet madness every morning clean.
Bearded, it waits for me at night.
How many lives I'll undo making you a distant country.
The hills could burn and with them the farmers and the farms.
When I say your name, I say the whole alphabet of my remembering.
God has three letters too but cannot spell
                      a moment of my happiness.

Memories are less imaginary—
placing them on Winchester at that window with your face,
waving them in wind that climbs my arm among the trees—
they are inches light and numbered as waves. Smiles are lakes
of bright blue upwards. My sleep, thin as abacus wire—
a dream of the body
                 that inhabits the body.

Each day a map of smoke, and I place you in it.
Where you are even has a name: *Oregon*.
The word sounds like forever
ago in my mouth.
               I call it the end of the world.

WHAT I TELL MYSELF

When I entered her, I was apologizing
to you. My tongue on her spine
spelled your name that was slipping
between the night and my teeth. The truth is

I was fixing my heart against yours.
With the drapes swimming with the moon.
When her back was the slope of a horse's nose
in a dark pasture in Tolono, I was kneeling
inside the chapel of you. And here

I don't know what to say.
There was no dream when we finished—

        my want, a pear tree bare against a wall
and a bird sewing the night shut with your name.
Hear me, it says.

AT THE BAR

A woman grates blood orange over rye,
her eyes like cool air coming through the door
of a motel room on a state highway
where two lawn chairs lean against a green wall.
A coffee can of wet cigarettes
at midnight in Des Moines. I am leaving
the small bathroom, undressing, lying
on the starch-stiff sheets with a beer
watching her slap her sandal against the heel of her right foot
where maybe she is singing in the doorway & waiting
for the starlight of her ash to die out,
or saying over the TV, *That was a long day,*
& with so much country on either side of us
we might remain here, rehearsing restlessness, forever
living lives by the hour
till whatever green language the room speaks
in the morning shows us where the world goes in waking.
If the streetlight is something I finger on her thigh,
then loneliness becomes a problem of forgetting—
the last four women I stood in front of naked,
their softness pressing into me like light into a curtain.

I am mid-life on a Monday in February; it is getting late.
She gives me what she's made on the rocks
& her smile is a wine glass hung by the foot
of its stem, quivering slightly
after having been put away.

46.7324° N, 117.0002° W

Where pines are druids in gray robes & November
closes like a fist on the sun at 4:30   I've left three letters
under everything My tongue   the colorless grass
the ridgeline staggered

like the back of some prehistoric thing crawling the dusk
in a painting of the Sawtooths   I've felt them
in the crushed wings of bats   in rain darkening a piano
in a garden   in the piano itself
outside the jail or the drughouse or the house
with the chicken coop Look

I can only tell you how empty the West is & full
of your name How I risked it   to the white pines
to the kitchen floor with my fists
Any direction I walked for years   was toward you
I have to stand still now Let joy be
the contortionist

I was even given the number of a psychic once
She wouldn't tell me how I was going to die
but if I said a name she'd tell me
about that person in my life   Some things

terrify My mind
slowed like a roulette wheel on the phone
when she asked mine   I wonder if she knew I'd changed it
to yours   so I could still hear it

WEDDING ON THE CLIFFS OF FORT WORDEN

Rain and the Cascades watermark Washington.
The tide coming in. A man's voice shaking
under a Madrone whose trunk is a wine-red tongue.
I'm amazed at the surety of the Word—
the vows reaching me in the grass.
The ferry passes west again, a boat slackens its sail.
How much of the world moves toward us
in increments—eyelashes, clouds, and wakes?

There is something about eternity that suffuses dusk.
The bride twirls like a carousel on the cliff, but not exactly.
It is quiet except for Rainier lighting the south,
its peak licked with birdshit—salt-runnels on a roof, the snow.
The napkin of evening folded gold by a plate.

We almost got married once. But I moved
in the dark toward the world's arms.
Held nothing going there.

46.7324° N, 117.0002° W

A bird's breath of twisted light
combs the porch   I call whatever blasphemy
to the dusk & drink dark beer
The altar of March answers me
with cold that shuttles the junked dreams of hills

I wait in a doorway
For what   Something anxious in me
coveting clouds or widows   asleep on roofs like rain
The park I pass heavy   closed with shadow

If I say *Starlight unanswered like a phone*
I am standing in the gangway where sleep has gone
idling in the moondiscs of moneytrees
in the alleys of mosspainted branches

Walk with me further   Cameron
do you take this clocktower in the dark to be your answer—
twice its creamed peal says the moon
is a koan   you'll forget You are talking
to yourself   There is no recourse

I am dialing the number of a dead friend
letting the signal busy my apology *Everything is still*
here I say   *except the world*
has gone to jail

If I say *Our minds*   I mean *How far apart*
If I say *A tree with birds*   I mean *My body*
If I say *Your loss sings*   I mean *Back to me*

MEDITATION ON SELF AND SLEEPLESSNESS

I used to spend the blue of my eyes like money
on things I wanted. Now,
the only color at 6,000 feet is the slowing of autumn.
Higher up, already winter in the Pioneers,
        the mountain and night sky
                        trash-bag dark and holding.

The moon pared like an apple. Wind rising.
Clothespins pinched to a line like butcherbirds.
It is late, I am watching odd gestures in the yard.
                        A dog barks down the valley.

Today, I wrote my charcoal shadow,
abandoned attempts at sleep. Dug from coals
at my feet with a bird that wouldn't shut up.
Carmine at first light, I watched him north
                        to something only he could see.

Silence and so much language is the privacy
of being human. I try with a cigarette
on the porch to make light. Where is God's
camouflage on a Monday night?
                        The old ways are bankrupt—

I don't want to celebrate myself, or live in America.
I don't know why it's easier to passively love
than actively forget. Why
the green regions are gone in the year. The yard. The eyes.
                        My mind's meringued.

But I'm here,
persistent in the world. It is something
to listen for yourself between the chest and sky.
Love too is starting with nothing but an idea.
I can be loved. Can't you

                    see the way the darkness looks at me?

44.6336° N, 86.2345° W

The moon through the pines says shadow
Means my eyes are Gaelic for dark walls   A woman is
combing her hair behind the curtains
in a small house   Her life
warm & yellow   My memory
drinks her sugarsense of hummingbirds

I am the language of nocturnals
Four decades old & whatever reflection the wind ruins
To the dark I say my chest   upon anything a sunken ship
My weight a boatful of irises   on Inishmore

I can see it I am the shadow   a dog chases I am the dog
Like the ripple of dark water
in a horse's eye I cannot sleep through the night
the month the century

The wind dies too
leaves stillness in the cathedral of Michigan
I think I am   become a watercolor
windows of my insides painted rain   Thirty years ago

I wrote my name in sand not far from here   erased it with my foot
You are three dreams away   When I understood my mind
I lived here
beautiful & with such little resistance

Notes

The epigraph to "Forest Exercises" is from W.S. Merwin's "Psalm: Our Fathers."

The epigraph to "Mythos" is from Yannis Ritsos's "Almost a Conjurer," translated by Nikos Stangos.

"William Blake & The Eternals" takes its title from Van Morrison's "You Don't Pull No Punches, but You Don't Push the River" from the album *Veedon Fleece*.

In "Compendium For Keeping It Together," the italicized line "*It is not your right to feel powerless*" is from Carolyn Forché's poem "Return."

The epigraph to "The Orphan" is from Sylvia Plath's "Lesbos."

In section II. of "The Orphan," "Behan's famine memorial" refers to John Behan's National Famine Monument sculpture in Murrisk, County Mayo.

Acknowledgements

My thanks to the editors of the following publications, in which certain of these poems, often in earlier versions, first appeared:

The American Poetry Review, Beloit Poetry Journal, CutBank, Fogged Clarity, Grist, The Harvard Advocate, La Presa, The Meadow, Measure, Mid-American Review, Raleigh Review, RHINO, Sonora Review, Terrain. org, Third Coast, Willow Springs, and *Western Humanities Review.* A special thank you to the staff at Willow Springs Books, who published a number of these poems in my chapbook, *Meridians.*

This book exists because of so many peoples' minds, poems, kindness, and generosity. My love and gratitude:

Michael McGriff, for your friendship and guidance, and for the July '17 poem-a-day, where many of these experiments began; Robert Wrigley and Alexandra Teague, for bringing me to the University of Idaho and for changing my life with poems; Brian Blanchfield, for the care and encouragement you gave this book; my University of Idaho MFA family, with special thanks to Nat Fisher, Michael Landreth, Garrett Chavis, Ash Goedker, Canese Jarboe, Corey Oglesby, Kat Lewis, Stacy Boe Miller, CMarie Fuhrman, Caitlyn Curran, Lauren Yarnall, and Ryan Downum; the New York State Summer Writers Institute, Port Townsend Writers Conference, and Fishtrap, where many of these poems were written; thank you Vijay Seshadri, Campbell McGrath, Dana Levin, and Joe Wilkins, for helping these poems find their way; Charlie Koltak, Rodrigo Palma, and Daniel Johnson, for bringing so much beauty, melody, and wisdom to my life: thank you for making records with me; my Chicago family, for everything; Brian Siers, Samantha Williams, Katie Darby Mullins, Elizabeth Renker, and Dave DeCastris, for your friendship and support over the years; Jericho Brown and Dorianne Laux, for kindly supporting this book; Kate Angus at Augury Books, for your generosity with and attention to these poems, and Joe Pan at Brooklyn Arts Press, for your support of this book and for bringing me into the Augury/BAP family: I'm grateful to you both for your guidance and kindness; Maggie Queeney, Battlecat, and Skeletor, for letting me join your pride, and MQ for reading this book with care so many times; my family; and you, dear reader.

About the Author

Cameron McGill is a poet and songwriter from Champaign, Illinois and the author of *Meridians* (Willow Springs Books). His poems have appeared in *The American Poetry Review, Beloit Poetry Journal, Grist, Raleigh Review, RHINO,* and *Western Humanities Review.* He has released seven albums, most recently *The Widow Cameron.* He teaches at Washington State University, where he serves as co-director of the Visiting Writers Series. He lives in Moscow, Idaho.

CPSIA information can be obtained
at www.ICGtesting.com
Printed in the USA
BVHW080314090221
599419BV00001B/73